CRAZY PLANT LADY

CRAZY PLANT LADY

ISABEL SERNA

Workman Publishing · New York

ISBN 978-1-5235-0537-1

Book design by Kat Millerick

Author photo: Mimoli Photography

Workman books are available at special discounts when purchased in bulk for premiums and sales promotions as well as for fund-raising or educational use. Special editions or book excerpts can also be created to specification. For details, contact the Special Sales Director at the address below, or send an email to specialmarkets@workman.com.

Workman Publishing Co., Inc.
225 Varick Street
New York, NY 10014-4381

workman.com

Printed in China
First printing February 2019

10 9 8 7 6 5 4 3 2 1

Thank You

to my family, my friends, and my love
for their unconditional support.

And to my mom, who is the
ultimate crazy plant lady.

crazy plant lady

noun \ krā-zē plant lā-dē \

1. A woman who has an insane,
almost addictive love for plants

2. A woman who has 10 or more
plants and gives them names,
talks to them, and thinks
of them as her children

3. A woman who finds pure
happiness in her plants

MILK

What I should be
spending my
money on

What I'm actually spending my money on

3 types of

CRAZY PLANT LADIES

ROSIE

- KNOWS EXACTLY WHAT TO DO
- MAINTAINS PERFECT PLANTS WITHOUT EVEN TRYING
- EVERY PLANT LADY WANTS TO BE HER
- HAS "THE GIFT" OF A GREEN THUMB

JASMINE

- ALWAYS ASKS FOR ADVICE
- VERY DISCIPLINED IN THE ART OF KEEPING HER PLANTS ALIVE
- CONSTANTLY KEEPS AN EYE OUT FOR LOW-MAINTENANCE PLANTS
- STRUGGLES WITH SOME PLANTS

VIOLET

- ROUTINELY NEEDS TO BUY NEW PLANTS TO REPLACE DEAD ONES
- DOESN'T KEEP TO A REGULAR WATERING SCHEDULE
- KILLS MOST OF HER PLANTS
- DOESN'T MIND GIVING FAUX PLANTS A CHANCE

you know you're a
CRAZY PLANT LADY
when...

Soup

Lavender Candle

every container is repurposed
as a planter.

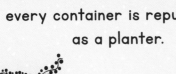

ALOE
you
VERA
much

BEING GOOD AT PROPAGATION

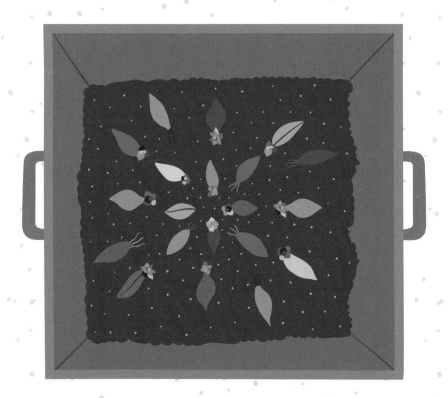

#Propagationstation

#ShelfieGoals

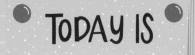
TODAY IS

#MonsteraMonday

URBAN JUNGLE
houseplants
BOTANICAL

I REMEMBER
TO WATER
MY PLANTS
MONSTERA
TIME

you know you're a
CRAZY PLANT LADY
when...

PLANT lady

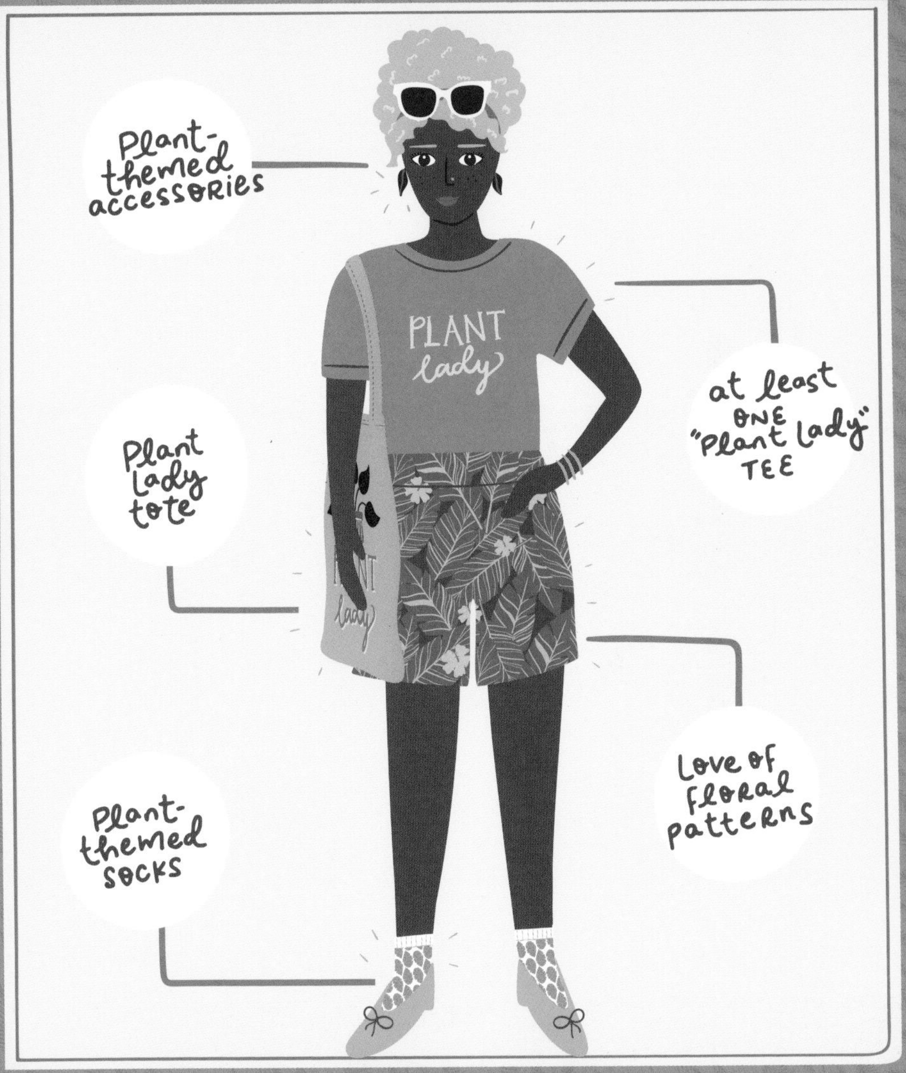

Plant-themed accessories

Plant lady tote

Plant-themed socks

at least ONE "Plant lady" TEE

Love of FLORAL Patterns

PLANT lady

MARIANNE NORTH
was the original plant lady!

During the late nineteenth century, North traveled the world by herself—often braving difficult terrain and primitive living conditions—in search of rare and undiscovered plants, which she then painted on the spot. One genus and four species are named in her honor.

ARE you A good PLANT MOM?

	YES	NO
Do you have a plant sitter on speed dial?	☐	☐
Do you keep to a strict watering schedule?	☐	☐
Have you mastered the art of propagation?	☐	☐
Do you have names for your plants?	☐	☐

	YES	NO
Do you rescue plants found on the street?	☐	☐
Do you talk/sing to your plants?	☐	☐
Are plants your #1 home decoration?	☐	☐
Do you know the likes and dislikes of all your plants?	☐	☐
Do you think about your plants when you're away?	☐	☐

every day
IS A
GOOD DAY
TO GO
PLANT
shopping

FIND THE CACTUS

phytomania

noun \ fɪ'tō-'māɪnēə \

AN EXCESSIVE OR UNBRIDLED
ENTHUSIASM FOR
COLLECTING PLANTS

THE MOST POPULAR FLOWERING POTTED PLANT IN AMERICA

is the

POINSETTIA

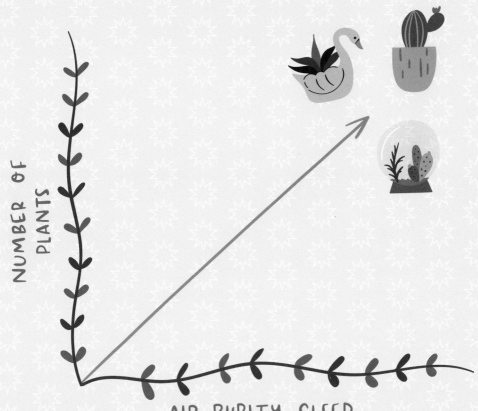

NUMBER OF PLANTS

AIR PURITY, SLEEP,
ENERGY, WELL-BEING,
BETTER SKIN

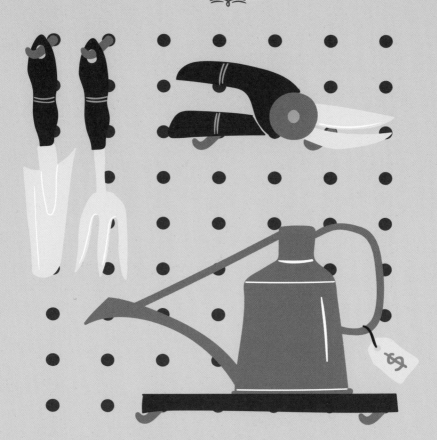

Buying ALL the cute planters and potting tools

PLANT LADY
DREAMS

Thrifting the perfect
vintage mister

¢50

Encyclopedia

OLD BOOK

you are stuck with me

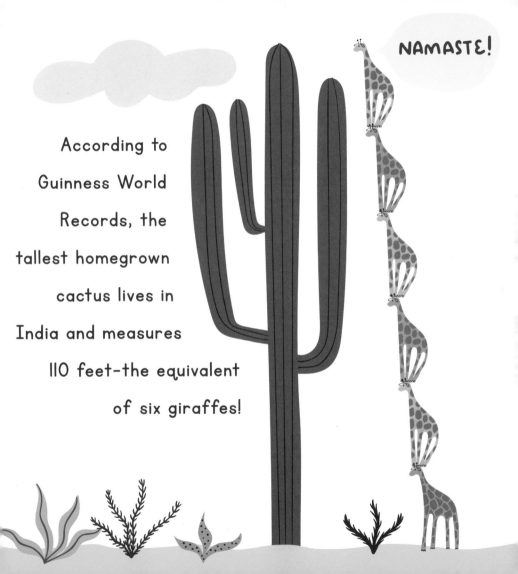

ANATOMY

of a

CRAZY PLANT LADY
BRAIN

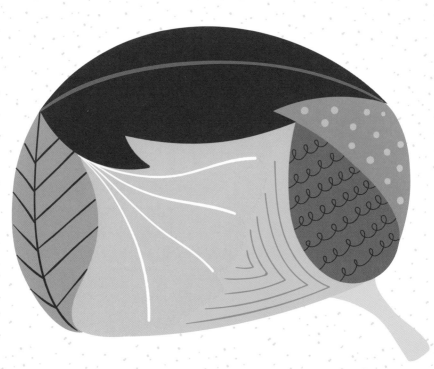

Buying more plants

 Watering schedules

 Finding cute planters

 Managing plant budget

 Taking photos of plants

 Everything else

benzene

carbon dioxide

Plants are green superheroes
who fight mold and bacteria for you!

dust spores

nitrogen dioxide

57

Plant Lady IS THE NEW Cat Lady

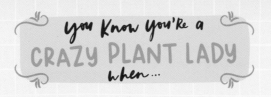

You Know You're a
CRAZY PLANT LADY
when...

you're planning a vacation and the first
thing you do is figure out who will take care
of your plants while you're away.

VACATION TO DO

- ☑ Water plants
- ☐ Who will water my plants?
- ☐ Pack

PLANT lady

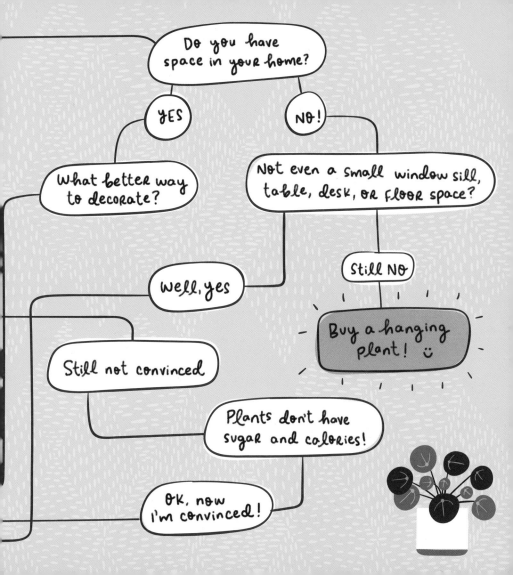

I LOVE
plants
MORE THAN
I LOVE
people

THINGS
A CRAZY PLANT LADY SAYS

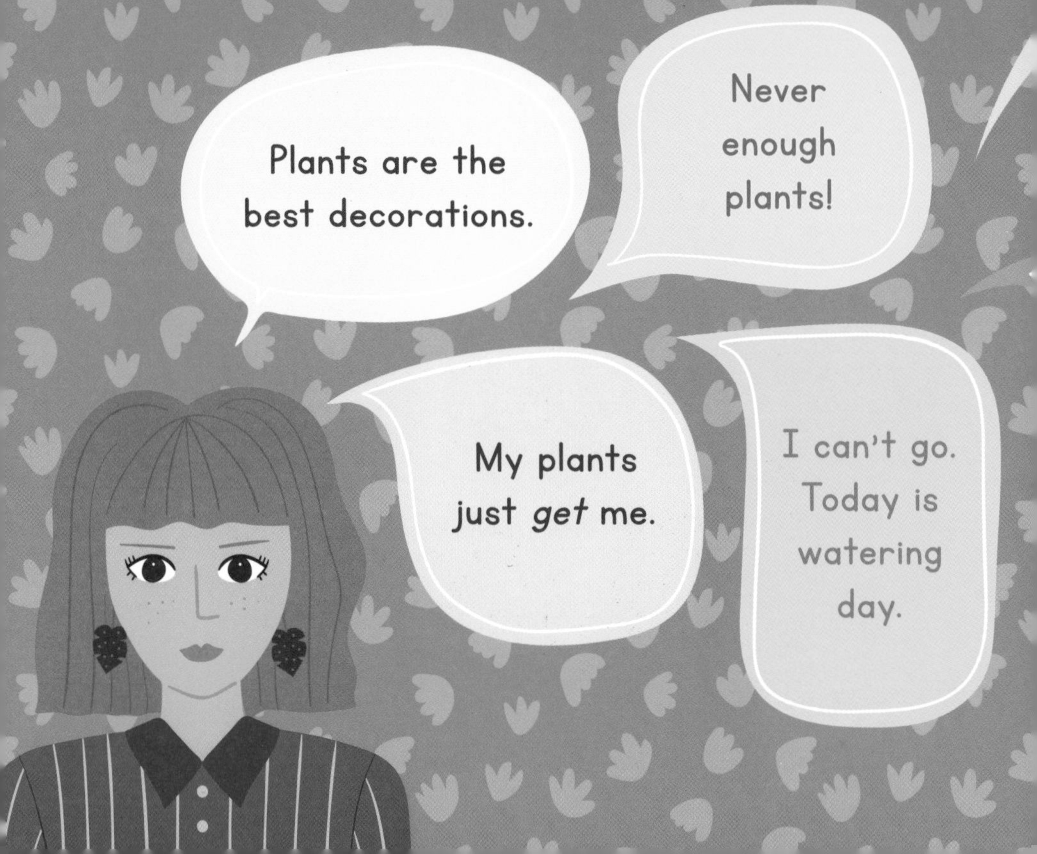

If you don't talk to your plants, YOU are the crazy one.

Being a crazy plant lady is a lifestyle.

Spike is looking happy in his new home.

Do you want to see how much Florence has grown?

I need a bigger house for my plants!

TODAY
is
#WateringWednesday

IMPORTANT

THE STRUGGLE
IS REAL

69

I GOT DIRT ON YOU

Saturdays are for repotting plants!

every available surface in your home serves as a plant stand.

Who needs curtains anyway?

NORMAL PLANT LADY

CRAZY PLANT LADY

I LOVE HANGING WITH YOU!

THE STRUGGLE IS REAL

OVERWATERING

82

UNDERWATERING

I'M QUITE FROND OF MY PLANTS

even your office is a jungle.

TODAY IS

SansevieriaSunday

A snake plant (Sansevieria Trifasciata) is also called Mother-in-Law's Tongue because of its pointy leaves.

crazy plant lady FRIENDS are the best KIND OF friends

You Know you're a
CRAZY PLANT LADY
when…

you have tons and tons of
plant-themed stationery.

i love
you
almost
as
much as
i love
my
fiddle-leaf
fig

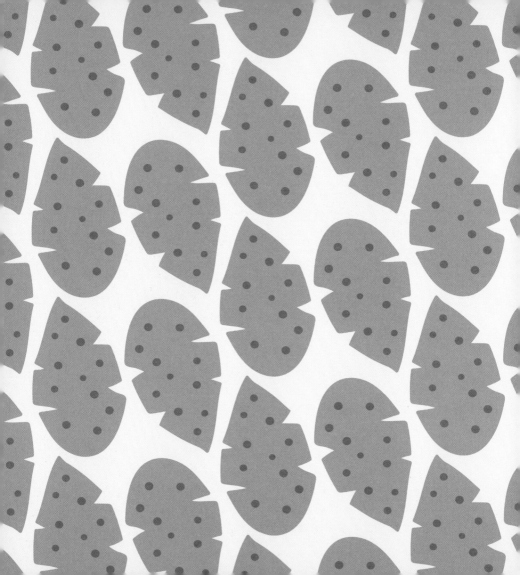

Monstera deliciosa is also known as a "Swiss cheese plant" because of the holes in its leaves.

you are my BEST fern

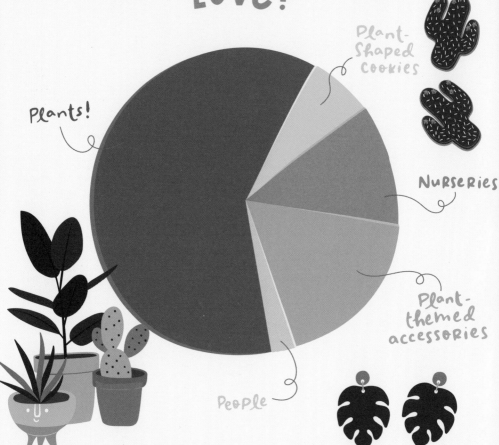

WHAT DO CRAZY PLANT LADIES LOVE?

Plant-Shaped Cookies

Plants!

Nurseries

Plant-themed accessories

People

About the Author

Isabel Serna is the founder of Black Lamb Studio, a Miami-based design studio with a focus on colorful patterns, illustration, fun stationery, and product design.

Formally trained as an industrial designer, her work can be found on wallpaper, wrapping paper, textiles, stationery, and various printed media. She has collaborated with brands such as Kate Spade, Hallmark, Travelpro, Mixbook, West Elm, and Figo Fabrics.

She lives with her husband, Juan, her French bulldog, Charlie, and many plants in Miami, Florida.